MW01531383

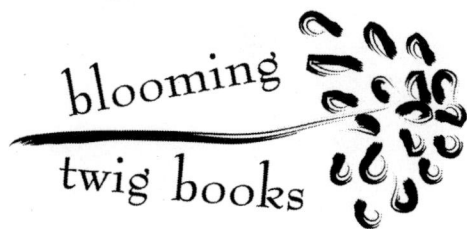

2006

blooming
twig books

WWW.BLOOMINGTWIGBOOKS.COM

Other Books by Cynthia Blomquist Gustavson

Poetry

Sick-A-War Tree

The Battle Within

I Don't Write Love Poems

Scents of Place

Ruach

Poetry Therapy

In-Versing Your Life: A Poetry Workbook
For Self-Discovery and Healing

Fe-vers: Feeling Verses for Children

Fe-vers: Feeling Verses for Teens

Re-Versing the Numbers: A Poetry Workbook
For Eating Disorders

Re-Versing Your Pain: A Poetry Workbook
For Those Who Live With Chronic Pain

Spirituality

Human Spirit, Holy Spirit

Kingdom Words

www.cynthiagustavson.com
www.bloomingtwigbooks.com

CON-VERSING WITH GOD

Poetry for Pastoral Counseling and Spiritual Direction

Poetry and Text by
Cynthia Blomquist Gustavson, MSW, LCSW, ACSW

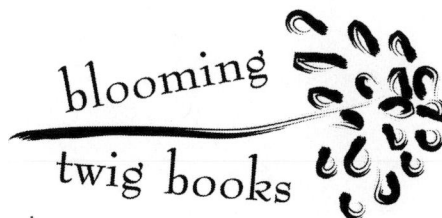

blooming twig books

NEW YORK

Several poems in this manuscript have previously appeared in <u>Scents of Place: Seasons of the St. Croix Valley</u>, by Cynthia Blomquist Gustavson. Published by Country Messenger Press, Marine on St. Croix, MN, copyright ©1987.

Several poems in this manuscript have previously appeared in <u>Where the Wind Comes From,</u> by Cynthia Blomquist Gustavson. Published by Holden Press, Tulsa, OK, copyright ©2001.

Several poems in this manuscript appear in <u>In-Versing Your Life</u>, <u>Ruach,</u> <u>The Battle Within</u>, <u>I Don't Write Love Poems</u>, and <u>Sick-a-War Tree</u>, by Cynthia Blomquist Gustavson. Published by Blooming Twig Books, Stony Brook, NY, copyright ©2006.

Con-Versing With God copyright ©2006 Cynthia Gustavson. Tulsa, Oklahoma.
www.cynthiagustavson.com
Published 2006 by Blooming Twig Books
3A Detmer Road
East Setauket, NY 11733
www.bloomingtwigbooks.com
Catalog #: BT004

9 8 7 6 5 4 3 2
First Blooming Twig Books Edition 2006.

ISBN-10 1-933918-00-04
ISBN-13 978-1-933918-00-4

All rights reserved. This book may be photocopied for personal or professional use only. No part of this book may be otherwise reproduced, stored in a retrieval system, or transmitted in any form or by any means (electronic, mechanical, photocopying, recording, or otherwise) without permission in writing from the author or publisher.

CONTENTS

INTRODUCTION

I am a pastoral counselor and poet, and so I have used poetry in my sessions since I first began counseling in 1984. I find that people who are walking a spiritual path relate well to poetry and metaphor. A particular poem can be used as a starter for individual or group discussions. It can also be used to gently jump start an individual to write his/her own poetry, which can be very self-revelatory.

All of the Biblical passages in this book use inclusive language. I find that it is extremely important not to alienate any persons, and using inclusive language is one of the ways to do that.

Feel free to copy any of the poems or exercises for your clients so that they may take them home and work on their writing in a private place. Ask them to bring their writing to the next session, and then discuss what they have discovered. You, and they, will be amazed.

I hope you enjoy the poetry and exercises. Poetry has been a lifesaver to me, and I am blessed to be able to share it with others.

Peace, Cynthia Gustavson

I. GOD, TELL ME WHO I AM

And I will be your parent, and you shall be my sons and daughters.

2 Corinthians 6:18

Dear Parent God,

Everyone else seems to know who they are. Why don't I? Am I my mother's daughter, or my daughter's mother, or my husband's wife, or my community's volunteer or my workplace's irreplaccable employee? Who am I as a child of God?

Amen.

Four Generations of Women

Grandma Anne's nimble hands
wove yarn into sweaters
the "old country" way,
no wrist movement, yarn caught
and held by taut fingers.

She wove it tightly, smoothly,
always her pattern in mind
knitting together the sometimes opposite twists
for cable or ribbing.
We learned it her way.

My mother chose not to knit—
used her fingers and fingernails
to fashion hair,
her pattern always in mind
combing together the sometimes opposite twists
for braid and roll.

I knit a little—
try to avoid my hair—
but write poems tightly, smoothly,
always my pattern in mind,
twisting words into braids, cables,
sometimes warm as Icelandic wool,
sometimes snarled and broken.

My daughter too has learned to knit
in a smooth, wristless fashion,
but her pulling is tight,
and her color-patterned sweaters buckle
beneath the weight of yarns carried behind.

❀

Family of Origin

What is the thread that knits your family together? Has it become unraveled? What kind of yarn (wool, angora, cotton, linen, synthetic) is your family knit from? Are you like your family or different? What does your family of origin tell about you? Did you grow up in the church? What effect did that have on you? What words or phrases do you still hear your mother or father saying to you? Are they helpful or harmful? Is it helpful or harmful to visualize God as father? Why or why not?

Write a poem in the form of a curvy piece of yarn called *Yarns Carried Behind.*

Catbird 1609C

The science man waits.
He says Catbird 1609C
will fly into the net
at the center left of the
right quadrant at half past
four today, as it does every
year in its migration north.

I laugh,
not because I don't believe
but because I've always known.

My Grandmother has walked
into Cannon Valley Church
every Sunday at nine thirty
for nearly ninety-two years,
knelt in the soil of her rose bed
on the first crisp days of May,
gathered her garden raspberries
by the nineteeth of July.

Mother, too, knows her place
under the trees her hands
planted half century ago,
trees that shade her farm,
their arms surrounding
spring fiddleheads of fern,
wild ginger, foam flowers
and deep growing bloodroot.

The science man waits.
Could this be the year
Catbird 1609C does not come —
by either death or choice
does not follow the river north
to the same meadows and nest?

Grandmother prunes roses.
Mother waters wildflowers.
The science man knows
when his birds will arrive
within seconds of time
and milliliters of space,

while I laugh —
and move to the city,
placing my belongings
in a car full of cardboard boxes
leaking black soil from slips of lily
and tiny plants of strawberry
that will grow to be everbearing.

Who Am I?

Are you more a product of "nature" or "nurture?" Can you remember when you were a child? Are you like that child, or has the world changed you? Have you ever felt that God's spirit changed you or even helped you remain who you are? What is important to you? Do you feel that everything is pre-ordained (like the habits of Catbird 1609C), or do you feel that you are free to make choices? Are you becoming the person you want to be, and/or the person you feel God wants you to be?

Write a poem called *What's Growing in the Black Soil?*

Timeless

Summers seemed eternal
The year my lithe body
Turned nine.

Solitaire and coloring
Within the lines of
Coloring books

Took up time, but not easily,
So I wandered worn
Paths of deer

And raccoon, thinking
They might lead
Somewhere.

I found sprays of wild
Black raspberries,
Stayed all day,

Picked amidst the thorns,
Then traipsed home
With cheeks

And hands stained
From berries and
Blood.

Summers now seem to
Disappear as easily
As deer

In the city. Maybe I
Should try solitaire
Again,

Make each day drag by
In waiting-in-line
Time

Or paint by number
Someone else's
Art.

Instead I follow paths
On yellow paper
Pads

And find phrases of wild
Description. I pick
And choose

Words amidst confusion,
Slowing time
Enough

To write them into poems,
Arriving home
With

Tattooed fingers stained
From ink and
Age.

Finding Time

Self-discovery takes time. So does walking a spiritual path. How do you find time for these important activities that are so often unappreciated by others? Do you have a special time each day set aside for meditation or prayer? Do you have a special place? How do you let others know its importance to you? Can you find a balance in your life between work, family, community and your own spiritual pilgrimage?

Pretend you are a pilgrim about to board a spiritual ship. What will you bring with you? What will you leave behind? How long will your journey be? Write a poem entitled *Embarking*.

12

Reinventing
(for Ed)

These wheels cannot go where he needs to go, wheels narrow
as bicycle tires, but not free wheeling, not free, as his legs used to be.
These wheels hold a chair, pushed only on flat surfaces,
not weedy places of tall grass or ascending rugged rock.

These wheels cannot take him into Redbud Valley,
where gnarled roots and sharp boulders block access
to the new boardwalk path, designed by an Eagle Scout
who doesn't know anyone who cannot walk.

Other wheels drive him home, past planted azaleas,
dogwoods, neat beds of pansies, bright reds and yellows
of cultivated plants, dark green fertilized lawns,
the yawns of Sunday sitters, and chatter of house sparrows.

These wheels cannot go where he needs to go,
to gushing cave springs rushing down rock,
beyond city-paved trails where others politely smile,
move out of the way, and are secretly glad it isn't them.

But they don't know this: That even the feel
of smog-filled wind or the sound of a simple sparrow's song
jogs the joyful memory of the rush of wild running,
the whoosh of his blood, the hush of his hurried mind.

How I've Changed

This poem was written for my husband, Ed, after a car accident that put him into a wheelchair for the rest of his life. Most of the changes that occurred in his life were obvious. But no one really understood one of the big changes, that he could no longer visit wild places, only places that were paved. It continues to be a painful loss.

How have you changed in ways that no one else knows? Are they good changes or not? Are they painful or joyful? Was God present in the change? What does a simple sparrow's song tell about you? Write about it.

Changed, Rearranged

Spirit

Spirit, we find your spirit divine,
we find your spirit in the flowers that grow.
Spirit, we find your spirit divine,
we find your spirit in the waters that flow,
in the apples, and the maples,
in the leaves that are turning orange and brown,
your spirit, your spirit, your spirit ever tumbling down.

Spirit, we find your spirit divine,
we find your spirit in our work and play.
Spirit, we find your spirit divine,
we find your spirit in the everyday,
in the dishes, and the wishes,
in the words we speak with loving care,
your spirit, your spirit, your spirit is everywhere.

Spirit, we find your spirit divine,
we find your spirit in the words of a friend.
Spirit, we find your spirit divine,
we know your spirit will never end,
in the vespers, and the whispers,
in the words of love that you extend,
your spirit, your spirit, your spirit's in the everyday wind.

❅

Where Do I Begin My Pilgrimage?

This song was written for a women's retreat about ten years ago. The women weren't surprised that they could find God, as well as their own spiritual selves, in the small things of life, in "the dishes and the wishes, in the words that we speak with loving care."

Begin your quest at home, in the "everyday wind." Look around. Where do you see God? Where do you feel God's presence? Write a poem entitled *Your Spirit Ever Tumbling Down*.

II. GOD, WHAT AM I TO DO?

Be strong and of good courage, and act. Do not be afraid
or dismayed; for God is with you.

1 Chronicles 28:20

Dear God of Infinite Wisdom,

I've read and studied your word, and attended church all my life. I've listened to my elders. I've read the philosophers and poets. But I still seek wisdom, wisdom for this moment in history, wisdom for my life in the midst of family and community. These poems reflect my questions.

Amen.

The Elegant Prophet

Her world – rouge and matte, hair highlighted, curled
with chemicals of peppermint, conditioned to shine,

no eating locusts, no flowing peasant robes,
rather hundred dollar wine and wraps of silk.

Who listens to a rebel, old-fashioned, unwashed?
Only a woman of her ilk attracts newsmen to her side.

Inherited wealth and hefty church donations
qualify her as spiritual guide, and give meaning.

She commands attention. Magnates and media listen –
I see them leaning to catch each precious word.

She points her painted nail and lifted chin
to the gathered herd. *It's there, you just have to take it.*

A woman with a child complains of lack of food.
An old man spits, muttering about being blind.

This prophet hears nothing as she leaves the stage
and media behind, and the light switches off.

❇

False Prophets

In the above poem a woman declares herself a prophet, and then does not live the life set forth by Jesus. Have you ever been misled by someone who calls himself/herself a prophet, a spiritual guide, or a minister of God? How do you discern who speaks for God? How do you know when God is speaking to you? Is it hard for you to criticize what a minister/rabbi/spiritual guide says? Do you believe they are called? How? Does that mean they do or say everything right?

Pretend that you have your own television program. What is one thing you know for certain that you can tell your audience about what God wants you to do with your life? Write your speech:

Ladies and Gentlemen . . .

Holy War

You do not have to forgive
spotted deer who nibble tender
leaves from your apple tree,
or corn-borers who devour
your sweet yellow ears,
or ants who march into your kitchen
as soldiers in a holy war.

You do not have to forgive
birds who nest in your chimney
or families of moles who
mound your manicured yard,
unless you value nature;
unless in hunger you have ever
picked and eaten a wild berry.

And you do not have to forgive
the drunkard who smashed
your favorite pottery turtle
against limestone boulders
in your rock garden, leaving
injured bloodroot and torn
hepatica to stand alone.

You do not have to forgive
that animal who left shattered
clay for you to find, broken
shards among the perennials,
unless you seek inner peace;
unless you have ever thrown
a valued vase against stone.

❧

Forgiveness

Do you seek inner peace? Have you ever lost your temper? Have you ever acted in a wild way? Then you must learn how to forgive yourself as well as others. Do it for yourself, or your future will be full of unhappiness and loneliness. There is not a soul alive who has never made a mistake. Try to understand what led up to the behavior in question. If you are unable to understand it, then you will have to learn to let it go another way. What does your religious belief system tell you about forgiveness?

Below are the letters of the word "mistake." Write a phrase beginning with each of those letters, and try to get around to forgiving, yourself or others, or asking for forgiveness, by the end of the poem.

M

I

S

T

A

K

E

Patience of the Cross Timbers*

Hundreds of years growing on a steep hill, desolate, aging
despite scarce nourishment, they wait for history to recognize them.

Crooked cedars, centuries old, twist in the shifting light of seasons,
and cling to a long forgotten hill shared by three-hundred-

year-old post oaks, every head cut off by lightning, every stump holding out
side limbs like wires on ragged and weathered clothes-line poles.

Recorded history reveals itself in the cross timbers' rings, some narrow
as a spider's thread, examined not by eye, but magnified to count

each period of drought, season of rain, each scarring fire, tornado, flood,
times of settlement and grazing. Washington Irving slept here

among the timbers, now a century older, and proclaimed them
beautiful. They have waited these years to hear it once again.

I wait. Transition is permanent. I understand these trees which grow
around rock and moss, trees which stretch limbs in crooked lines

seeking elusive light, trying to catch the run-away water, clinging to life
long enough to leave a legacy on the land before becoming

firewood. Their endurance, spirituality of patience, their
mandala of encyclopedic rings. What they have is what I want.

*Remains of the south central old growth forest, called the Cross Timbers, made up mostly of post oak
and red cedar ranging in age from 300 to 1000 years old, discovered in 1999 in Oklahoma.

Patience

Patience is a rare commodity in our times. Was there a time in your life when you had more patience, or less patience? Are you more, or less, patient with those you love? How about patience with yourself? Do you need the answer now, the money now, the relationship now? What does the phrase "Transition is permanent" mean? What does it have to do with patience? What are you waiting for? Have you ever thought about God's time?

Take your writing materials and go for a walk in nature. Sit against a tree trunk and wait. What do you hear? Smell? See? Touch? Sit for a long while before writing, then write what this experience of waiting silently felt like.

Unbearable

When my ears hear a whispered moan, the too loud crash
Of brakes and shattered glass, when muscles shudder
And wait for one more night of terror to pass

I cast off what is left into a deep, deep place
Where it twists and turns and will not hold still.

When eyes see the sigh of pain on my lover's face,
The struggle to grip, to walk, to regain *normal*,
When I am too full to witness one thing more

I cast off what is left into a deep, deep place
Where it twists and turns and will not hold still.

When my mouth tastes bitter words, the salt
Of exhausted service, when food has no appeal
And water, vinegar and wine seem the same

I cast off what is left into a deep, deep place
Where it twists and turns and will not hold still.

Pain

When you experience or witness pain, physical and/or emotional, does it bring you closer to God or alienate you? Do you have a deep, deep place where something painful is twisting and turning? Do you try to avoid that place? What would happen if you go there deliberately, God with you, and confront the pain?

Try going somewhere alone, maybe just inside your car in the garage, and screaming out the pain. Do not let it simmer inside you. Later, change that released "pain" into "paint" by taking markers or paints and drawing the pain in reds and ice blues, drawing it flowing away from you, draw it being taken in by God.

Song of a Norwegian Summer Day

The tow-headed boy pokes bushes for surprises,
tries to free a half-buried elk antler,
upsets an anthill to watch the scurrying,
picks berries not yet blue enough to eat.

He sings: la, la, loo, loo, loo, I am here
on this cold day of all-day-sun
the only one who remembers to have fun.
It is July. It is summer.

Gala Lake is clear as a window pane
outlined in gray granite, framed
with green mountain fir, and so cold
the bottom rocks themselves seem to shake.

Grandma sits and eats reindeer sausage.
Grandpa fishes from shore wearing hat and mits.
Father shouts for the boy to hush, but he
listens instead to the wind and the shaking rocks.

He sings, la, la, loo, loo, loo, I am here
on this cold day of all-day sun, and then
pulls off his socks, digs his toes in sand and
holds the antlers within his white, white hair.

Living the Moment

Do you often find that you have lost the day because you were fretting about yesterday or anxious about tomorrow? It's not easy to live as lilies of the field who "neither toil nor spin," or as the ravens who "neither sow nor reap." The little boy in the poem has the luxury to live each moment without worry. It was a joy to watch him, and to remind me that life is here to be enjoyed, to be felt, to be engaged in.

Where are you at this moment? (In a chair, a couch, at a desk, waiting for the doctor, relaxing during your child's naptime, enjoying a work break?) Wherever you are, stop. Take a deep breath. Hold it. Let it out slowly. Say the word "relax" as you let out the air. Relax all the muscles in your body. Now, what do you see, smell, feel, taste, hear? Engage in this moment as you have never done before. Is God beside you? Within you? What have you learned about God's creation?

Write about what you have experienced.

Step Around

Life ain't been no crystal stair.
Langston Hughes

They try to make it into a stair,
crystal or no,
tell us we're moving up,
we're on the way, a step ahead,
up another rung,
until we reach a plateau
and where do we go
from there?

I say
we don't need to climb a ladder,
or get high enough to fall,
all we need to do is walk
together on this
flat-on-the-ground circle
stepping around
stones, entering
doorways.

❦

Circle of Life

A wedding ring is a circle, no beginning, no ending. A hug is a circle. A year is a circle, spring, summer, fall, winter and again to spring. A pregnant woman's stomach is a circle, full of new life. Jump off your ladder if you are on one, and enter the flat-on-the-ground circle of acceptance and love.

Draw a circle on this page and draw in it all the important parts of your life, even those that others considered failures. This is your circle of life, sacred and beautiful.

32

At the Place of No Conversation

She visits often,
but understands
Lily does not know her,

her joyous smile steady
though there is no
greeting in return.

Returning is harder
with each trip
to the nursing home.

Home seems far away
at this place
of no conversation.

Conversation here
is rubbing lotion
on Lily's hand,

her hands stiff,
boney and always
cold,

her eyes too, cold, but
also wide-eyed,
bold.

With hope the visitor
brings this time
a guest.

Who would have guessed
what Sophie, the dog,
could sense?

Scent alone
does not explain
Sophie's nuzzling care.

Careful now,
she licks the palm
of Lily's hand,

handles her gently,
rubbing the old woman
with warm fur.

Furrows lift
from Lily's eyes.
Her lips curl to form words.

Wordless too long,
she grabs the glistening black
fur. Come Back.

How Do I Know God?

In your concept of the Divine are you open to thinking of God in many ways, not just as a father? In what ways is the Divine like a pet dog? In this poem the dog's name is Sophie. That is the name that represents Wisdom in the Bible. How is this "dog" wise? Does Lily break out of the "place of no conversation?"

One of the author's eight-year-old clients talked about God as a kitten who cuddled up to her at night when she was afraid and no one else was around. Martin Luther talked about God as a mighty fortress. Could God be like the river that carved out and flows through The Grand Canyon? Could God be an atom? Could God be compared to chocolate? Could God be a big breasted, jolly woman?

Write a list of metaphors that describe different aspects of God.

God is like ....

God is like ....

God is like..

God is like ....

God is like ....

III. GOD, TEACH ME HOW TO LOVE

Love is patient; love is kind; love is not envious or boastful or arrogant or rude. It does not insist on its own way; it is not irritable or resentful; it does not rejoice in wrongdoing, but rejoices in the truth. It bears all things, believes all things, hopes all things, endures all things. Love never ends.
1 Corinthians 13: 4-8

Dear God of Love,

Because you nourish us, we know the taste of love. Because you keep us in your strong arms,

we feel the safe, warmth of love. When we sing your praises we hear the melody of love.

When you gently redirect us, we know the discipline of love.

Keep us ever mindful of that love in all we think, feel and do.

Amen.

Something Stolen

Prisoners used to wear stripes,
(who cared if they defiled the zebra?)

but one too many must have run away
blending in with nature's cover.

Jails now send out work crews
in jumpsuits of neon orange

not matched in nature except in
Florida fruit and October maples.

That's why I bought the orange wool coat
that no one wanted, on sale for a year,

wool to warm the coming winter,
brightness to ward off approaching darkness,

reminding me of the orange heather suit
and angora sweater I wore the night we met,

bittersweet pinned in my cornsilk hair,
lipstick to match autumn's brilliance.

Now I wrap the warm coat around me
as I pick pyrocantha berries and hunt

orange mushrooms, remembering
not prisoners, but something stolen.

❧

Something Stolen, Lost, or Unattainable?

What are you missing in your life? Is it something that you used to have, or something you think everyone else has except for you? Is it an aching inside that tells you something is missing? Are you getting through each day because you are very, very busy, but when you quit the busy-ness you feel empty? Is it love you are missing? What kind of love? Friendship? Romance? An intimate relationship with God? Or is it that you feel that you lack meaning in your life? Do you wonder why you are on the earth?

These are stunning questions that demand answers. Are you trying to answer them using the tools you learned in childhood, and finding that they lead to dead ends? Think out of the box. Think about a God-size box.

Dig into your feelings. Use a God-sized, padded shovel and allow yourself to dig deeper than ever before. Write about what you find in this excavation:

I Don't Write Love Poems

Mom's advice: *Don't do what I did. Don't marry a musician.*
Romance never lived in a just-do-what-you-have-to-do house.

There's time to sleep when you're dead, Grandma said. Too tired,
both grandpas and Dad fell asleep when I was a teen.

I don't write love poems.

I write about flowers, zinnias and hollyhocks
Grandma planted beside her house, beside her shed

and when she needed more room she planted roses
where her neighbor's late wife used to plant petunias.

In return Mr. McKeig mended her fence, painted her porch,
mowed her grass, and kept her path clear in winter.

Until one night he died and Grandma, not knowing how to cry,
stopped eating, then called her family to her side,

said it was finally time for her to sleep. She died in peace
after giving instructions about how to care for her roses.

I don't write love poems.

I write about roses, white-painted porches,
shoveled walks on snowy days, a call, a smile.

❀

Love Your Neighbor as Yourself

Does love have to be romantic? Sexual? What does mature love mean? What does it mean to love your neighbor? What does it mean to love yourself? Do you always put yourself last? Is that what the scripture says? Or do you always put yourself first? Think about some of our heroes and heroines, (Martin Luther King Jr., Gandhi, Albert Schweitzer, Rosa Parks, Mother Theresa.) Even though we know they were human and had their faults, they displayed love in extraordinary ways.

Think of one time when a neighbor showed you love. Then think about a time when you showed love to a neighbor.

Take the letters in "Love your neighbor as yourself" and write down as many words as you can. Now write them into a poem about loving self and neighbor.

ring of love beads

in '68 we let our hair grow long, dangled love
beads over peasant blouses thin enough
to spy both skin and shadow

we knew they didn't give peace a chance
hadn't loved anything but money,
didn't know our kind of love

the kind you can't buy with commercial
smiles or money earned from their
military/industrial complex

dads threw us out while mothers cried
We tried our best, and sent cash
and letters signed *I love you*

it would never happen to our children, given
time and talk, books instead of guns,
not even sticks to aim

but they shave their heads, tattoo thigh
roses, hang rings from their noses
and use our language

to aim sharp words shot straight
as arrows into the target of our
ecological/wellness complex

can't party on baked potato chips
can't get rich writing letters
or reading books

i send cash for therapy and leave messages
on e-mail *did best i could*
love you, mom

�֎

Parent/Child Love

Whether you are a parent or child you have probably found out that loving the other is not always easy. One of the startling surprises of my life has been how deeply in love with my children I have been since their birth decades ago. What that kind of love inspires is a way of never letting go, even in the worst of circumstances. What is seldom taught in families, but should be universal knowledge, is that we need to always love the person, but not necessarily love the behavior of that person.

Write a poem in the form of an email message to a parent or child with whom you have had a problem. Is it possible to love them (in what way?) without loving the behavior? Write it in lower caps, the way emails are often sent. When "I" is "i" it reminds us to be humble.

Wings
For My Daughter's Wedding

Mandarin ducks, with golden wings and fluorescent feathers,
peck for seeds in my backyard and proclaim their territory.

Just to see them skips my heart. Part of my otherwise ordinary day,
they are extraordinary. A neighbor brought them from China.

Love, too, is unexpected, unexplained, sometimes a stranger,
but golden and fluorescent against plain grass and gray rain.

I tell myself they will never become plain old ducks, quacking,
waddling, making a mess, ordinary ducks I forget to notice.

And I wonder if they will always feel foreign in this aerated
American pond, finding no other fowl exactly like them.

I answer: Love's bond creates its own encompassed world.
Home is any wetland, swamp or manicured lake.

Love's brush paints us golden as these mandarin ducks
and brings out shimmers of exotic fluorescent blush.

It draws feathers light enough to both fly and float,
and with dark tones underlines the muscles of our wings.

❈

The Exercise of Love

The last line says that love is a paint brush and "with dark tones underlines the muscles of our wings." Why "with dark tones?" How do we get the "muscles of our wings?" How do we keep them? What is the work of love? Does this poem, which was written for my daughter's wedding, say that love is only "exotic fluorescent?" Write a list of things about love (married or otherwise) that require work. (You may want to refer to I Corinthians 13.) Most of us who work for a living work a 40 hour week. How many hours of work a week do we put in for love? What is the payoff?

Write a poem entitled *Earning A Loving.*

The Gift of Tomatoes

The old woman
comes with bags
of fruit, tomatoes
from her garden,
the taste sweet and
almost forgotten.
Unlike store bought,
they leave a pungent
odor in my hand.

A garden gift,
no matter how
often received,
is a lifting of each
round fruit, each
ripe moment, saying,
Take this. Eat.
Make it part of you.

❀

The Gift

Love is always a gift, never expected. Has it been freely offered to you, and you have been too afraid to accept it? Have you been hurt in the past and refuse to allow love into your heart again? Love is always a risk. It cannot guarantee against heartbreak. Love requires emotional intimacy. The choice is yours; isolation and safety (leading to loneliness,) or intimacy and vulnerability (leading to relationship and love.) The words in the poem, "Take this. Eat. Make it part of you," tell of the intimacy of love.

Imagine that Someone has given you a beautifully wrapped gift. Inside may be a bomb or a valuable jewel. What will you do with the gift?

Write a poem entitled *Unwrapping the Gift*.

48

You Know What I Wish?

Thanks for the oatmeal cooking since six,
For the nuts and berries you cut up and fixed,
The orange juice you squeezed, and the toast I see,
But what I want to know is: Do you love me?

My clothes are washed and folded and hung.
My sores are soothed when I'm cut or stung.
You get me to bed. You wake me up too,
But I want to know: Do you love me? Do you?

You tell me you love me but what does that mean?
Will you love me if I fail to keep my room clean?
Will you love me if I'm ugly, or if we never agree?
How am I s'posed to know if you really love me?

The dog wags his tail when I bring treats up the path.
My friend loves me 'cause I finish his math.
The cat only purrs when I put out her fish.
Do you know what I want? Do you know what I wish?

I want you to think of me when you see the sun rise,
To see me in your dreams behind the lids of your eyes,
To smile when I'm happy, to soar when I'm free.
And if you cry when I'm sad, then I'll know you love me.

❖

How Do I Know?

Even though this is a child in the poem who is asking the question, this is a universal question asked by every human being at some time in his/her life. Do you love me unconditionally? Does God love me unconditionally? Do you love others without condition? How do we prove love? Can it be proved by actions, or is it something that we feel? Review the people in your life who have loved you. How did you know it was real love?

List characteristics of real love, such as in the fifth stanza of the poem. Write a last stanza to this poem including your own observations of love.

He Loves Me . . .

only the yellow eye remains
as ox-eye daisy petals
are pulled out
       one
   by
one
to envision love

❀

The Vision of Love

Do you remember pulling out daisy petals? Did that exercise come up with the right answer? Is your vision of love different now from when you were younger? How has it changed? What did you expect of love then? What do you expect of love now? Has culture changed your expectations of love? Do you expect to love only one person for life? Do you agree or disagree with your church's teachings on marriage, divorce, and relationships? Why?

Write a contract with yourself about your expectations of a relationship:

I expect myself to…

I would expect my partner to…

It would be good if I …

It would be good if my partner …

IV. GOD, BE WITH ME AS I AGE

Now Abraham and Sarah were old, advanced in age; it had ceased to be with
Sarah after the manner with women. So Sarah laughed to herself, saying,
"After I have grown old, and my husband is old, shall I have pleasure?"
God said to Abraham, "Why did Sarah laugh? . . .
Is anything too wonderful for God?"
Gen 18:11-14

Dear God of Abraham and Sarah,

I know that to live is to grow older. I can't escape it, no matter how many vitamins I take or how much make-up or surgery I use. I wish I could laugh with joy, as Sarah did, when she was promised a child in her old age. Instead I am anxious about what I should have learned by now. I am anxious about my body growing older, about my senses growing dimmer, and my pace slowing. Help me to age gracefully, always keeping in mind your grace, your pace, and maybe a little accumulated wisdom.

Amen.

Before the Fall

Leaves not bright enough to notice,
none are down, yet days darken
and northern winds flip exposed fingers.

Today this leaf, supple, returns
as I squeeze its green body. Red
trims only the edge. Dry onion skin
remains weeks away.

I look closer.

Far outer tips have already blackened -
crisped like peppered catfish
in a Cajun skillet.

As night lengthens
life shortens.
Like nails clipped to the quick
death begins at the edges.

❋

Reading the Signs

What are the signs that you are aging? A little arthritis perhaps? Gray hair coming in? Cholesterol up? Belly rounder? We all know the signs of our physical entropy. But what about the signs of our spiritual aging, or could I call it ripening? As our bodies age we are given the opportunity to become wiser, to ripen. Is that happening with you? Are you closer to God? Do you see things in a different light? Do you judge less, and enjoy more? The poem says "death begins at the edges." Death to the old self? Death to the judgmental self? Death to the egotistical self? How are you growing wiser?

Draw a leaf on the page below and write in it what is dying, and what is thriving.

Rising Backwards

When I learned to write my name it slanted backwards.
Even when Teacher slapped my knuckles
the dancing flow of letters filled a space no other writer owned
and no teacher could persuade me to abandon.

Later in school I loved to study the reason ancient peoples
wrote on walls, and I loved to juggle geometric puzzles,
proving theorems back to their origin, where
thinking backwards was to my advantage.

When I bought my ten-speed bike I peddled backwards,
no gear to slow rotation, flowing up and down
like bubbling oil, but of course, the bike went nowhere,
only my feet were in orbit.

When I play tennis I win with a strong backhand.
Opponents try to outwit me by putting the ball behind,
but my mind is seldom in front
and my two-handed return is powerful.

I prefer the back of the bus where I feel the road beneath,
and the under-belly of my Victorian porch in the cool,
dog-haired dirt. It reminds me that the flip-side of life
is most certainly not death. It's more like

getting chained into a forward facing seat
of a double ferris-wheel and swiftly rising backwards
through enormous space, up and around, circling,
my face coming last, surprised and weightless.

❈

Self Esteem

Self-esteem may take a hit as we age. Women are often judged for their youthful beauty. Men are told that they must be energetic and creative to keep their jobs. If the world is telling us that we are becoming useless as we age, how do we counteract that characterization?

We must know our strengths and weaknesses, so that others cannot take advantage of our weaknesses, and we can rally our strengths when we need them.

Write a list of what others might call your faults. Choose one and write a poem about it, transforming it into something humorous, acceptable, or at least into something that is not deplorable to you. And remember, as in the poem "Rising Backwards," what you've been told is wrong or backwards about yourself may be (God-given) exactly right for you.

Exposing My Backside to the Sun

Dialysis

Century-old oak once again
time-determined dialysis drains, weakens;
your sinking sap recalls memories of torture.

In fall, flushed with color,
your warm, sweet sap now steals and stores
its verdant shade underground.

No longer soft, plump, your condition
exposes wind-writhing naked beauty,
acutely skeletal, but upward.

Now the owl
sleeps lightly
yet remains in faith

until the blizzard passes
the grasses return
and new life rises.

✂

To Everything There is a Season

Do you resent the past or fear the future? Are you a spring bud, a full growth of green canopy, a leaf flushed with fall color waiting to be noticed or to fall, or are you exposed to the north wind waiting for the blizzard to pass? Is God only in the spring bud, or only in the fall color? Is God in the blizzard as well? Within the cycle of life we also have growth cycles. What kind of dialysis could make your sap rise again?

Write a poem about where you are, and where you are heading. Call it *And New Life Rises.*

The Icebox

Her eighty-year-old heart beat like a captured bird
but she held him with a steady hand until help came.

That same body wiped his drool, spoke for him,
dressed and cleaned him, walked down aisles
old-slow with him;

With clenched jaw she learned his diagnosis, stood stiff
then smiled as she thanked the doctor
for his kindness;

With precision she packed pictures and pajamas
he'd need at the rest home, drove him there, settled him.

In her empty bedroom she held herself and said
it had to be—then slept a restless sleep—
three hours maybe.

Friends insisted, "Take care of yourself"
so she bought something new
to fill the emptiness,

But when the Sears men in gray jumpsuits
brought the new icebox to replace the old one

Her body shook with tears as she cradled
the used machine on its path
to the waiting truck;

And nothing they said and nothing she did
could stop the metal-on-metal
wrenching of the gears

As the years rolled backward onto the truck
until her steady hand let go.

Tomorrow she would tell him all about
the ice water in the door
and special compartments

But of course he knew of those—
and she would hold him
with a steady hand.

When I Can't Live in My Home Anymore

In this poem a conscientious wife takes care of her husband until she is unable to continue any more. She is full of grief and guilt at having to place him in a nursing home. How do you feel about nursing homes?

Have you asked your parents how they feel or what their wishes are? Have you told your children what your wishes are? What are the criteria to be used for such a decision? How does love speak to this situation? If you decide to down-size into senior housing or a nursing home, what will you give up?

Find a passage from scripture that supports you as you down-size your home, your life, your expectations, your freedom of movement, and your health. Rewrite it into your own words.

The Whole-Day-Life of a Lily

in memory of Sarah

Morning air falls cold
petals unfold
and settle in

She wonders where
she's at
but knows

To aim her stamen
and pistils into
interstitial space

Yellow gold
as the sun's face
bold as nuclear fusion

Soft as dawn
yellow gold, alert
against the green grass lawn

A butterfly tickles
gold on gold
waves wings to summon

Hummingbirds and insects
little girl's and
boy's "Oh's"

Her lily bell alert
welcomes them
even

When hurt
by rain, wind, child,
and chill

She stands
her one day
tall and still

Until day's end
then nods to what
has become her home

Nods to
the setting sun
the yellow gold sun

against a blackening sky,
and closes tight
her lily bell

Folding in petals
stamen and
pistils

And falls
gold yellow lying
on the green grass lawn

Evening air falling
on cold, fading petals
Gold sun gone

Which Way Am I Facing?

Toward the end of its one day life, the day lily in the poem "nods to the setting sun, a yellow gold sun, against a blackening sky." The lily follows the light, and only sees the yellow gold sun. The blackening sky is at its back. As we age do we follow the light, or succumb to the darkness? What does it mean to keep our face to the light, the "yellow gold sun"? (I John 1:7 *Walk in the light as he himself is in the light.*)

Write a traditional rhyming poem about where you are heading and where you are looking, and use words that rhyme with the word "sun." (fun, begun, won, one, run, done, ton, shun, redone, etc)

V.   GOD, COMFORT ME
IN THE FACE OF DEATH

But Ruth said, "Do not press me to leave you or to turn back from following you! Where you go, I will go; where you lodge, I will lodge; and your God will be my God. Where you die, I will die – there will I be buried. May the Almighty do thus and so to me, and more as well, if even death parts me from you."
Ruth 1: 16-17

God of Love,

People I love have died. It started with my father at 13, and my grandfather died the next year at my father's grave. My grandmother was buried the day before my wedding. Death. It is more than loss. It is finality. I have written hundreds of poems about my father's death. Though it was over 45 years ago, reading or writing about it still evokes sadness and tears. A canoe accident gave me a glimpse of my own death and it still makes me cherish each living moment. I continue to write about death because it reveals more about the life I am living. Guide me, and others, in that pilgrimage.

Amen.

What My Friend Told Me

I am eight years old and slipping on my boots
wondering whether the snow will melt
and lightning scorch the skies when
the world ends today.

Who set this date, sent out this warning
so all of us in the know are prepared,
like a girl scout working on a life badge
before the world will end?

And why are Dad and the neighbor
going to their jobs, the bus driver greeting
us with the same noble smile on this day
the world will end?

We all come to school unprepared
for our lessons. The teacher doesn't
understand. She says, *We won't know
the time when the world will end.*

We wait. My feet fidget up and down.
My fingers turn cold. I do not hear
what the teacher is saying. I am afraid
what will happen when the world ends.

I ride home on the bus, its wheels gripping
and slipping on the slick pavement. I know
it's coming as I push away my dinner which
I won't need when the world ends.

Mother asks why I'm not hungry as she tucks
me with a kiss into the bed in which
shortly I will spend my last moments
of terror when the world ends.

I fall asleep praying I will see Mother again,
and Teacher and Bus Driver, and snow and ice.
I awaken to the smell of eggs, broken and
frying in lard, yellow yolks hardening.

❧

What Will I Say to Death?

The child in the above poem believes that the world is going to end. Do you remember being afraid of that? Do you have dreams where you feel you are dying? What does that feel like? Is death the enemy? Is the process of dying frightening to you? What is your familiarity with death? Are you dying? A loved one dying? Close your eyes and visualize Death. Talk to it. What will you say? What will you ask?

Who will be at your side as you converse with Death? Do not be passive. Stand tall. Do not be aggressive. Listen to what it has to say to you. Be assertive. Ask your questions. Ask for help if you need it. Feel the strength of God at your side.

Write about this experience.

Paisley Dress of Purple

When she asked what I'd wear, I knew it would be paisley,
dark and wiggling fabric draped over my tight shoulders,

this fabric massaging flesh and something else
deeply wounded in my thirteen year old frame.

I love the shapes of paisley as they whirl and
twist, colors blending into the last light of sunset,

the almost-dark time when shades of purple spread
across the sky, creep into air and take over my breath.

I chose the paisley dress for father's funeral,
it's dim light all that was left of day.

❈

My Response to Death

The teenager in the poem did not want to give in to the blackness of death, and so she chose a paisley dress of purple to wear to her father's funeral. It reminds me of New Orleans funerals where the survivors refuse to remain mournful and play their extraordinarily upbeat, but spiritual, music in honor of the dead friend. How do you respond to death? Does death steal a little of you as well? If you are approaching your own death, how do you want to face it? How do you want others to respond to it? What kind of funeral (celebration) do you want? What music? What poetry? What scripture? Do you want it solemn, or lively?

Write down your wishes on this page and show them to your loved ones.

Autumn Bread

I bake bread
when outside temperatures fall
and leaves heat
to brick-oven hues—
when wild rice is pounded into boats
headed in curved lines
toward winter—

I bake wild rice baguettes
long and tough-grained

I boil the wild rice
twice as long as white
to get it soft enough for bread
soft as the loaves my friend's mother baked
soft as my mother's voice that morning
soft as tears

My bread is whole-grained
made of wheat-berry and wild rice

My friend's kitchen
always smelled of yeast—
same as mine does now—
but she was the wild addition—
We were both thirteen but it was
her skin and blood that matched
the autumn leaves in brilliance—
Father called her wild, didn't trust the
Irish in her

No Irish soda bread for them
her mother used yeast

Even the night he said "No"
when I stayed overnight anyway
the loaves were rising there—
and in her morning kitchen
as the telephone rang—
rising, as her mother's smile fell,
still rising, as she drove me quickly home

past brick-red oaks
beginning to brown

It was then all rising collapsed
with the trembling, controlled calm
of Mother's voice,
"Your father's gone—
He died last night—
You be strong, we'll make it"

My bread is tough-grained
hiding soft wild rice.

Death is Always Unexpected

Do you dread the phone call in the middle of the night? Is there ever any way to prepare for that? Do you fear that someone you love will die and you will not have reconciled some long-lasting disagreement? Are you afraid you will die and someone you love, who is vulnerable, will never recover? Death is always unexpected. We must always be ready. If you have not talked to someone in years, pick up the phone. Learn to say "I'm sorry," or "I'll listen." Learn to pray. Learn to forgive. Your bread may be tough-grained, but it doesn't taste good without the "soft wild rice." Does the thought of death allow you to act wildly? To act softly?

Write about the way you will prepare for your or others' deaths in a poem called *Headed in Curved Lines Toward Winter.*

Funeral

Organ pipes drone from the balcony
while youth laugh and chatter
not knowing how to feel.

Silent elders, dark as shadows,
replay stories in their minds
on black and white film.

They hear the laughter and fear
both present and future,
not realizing that joy

vibrates the holy space,
and shakes up created worlds.
Something dead is stirring.

❈

Something Must Die

In autumn leaves and grass die to be born again in spring. In Christianity we have Good Friday death and Easter resurrection. In our lives too a grandparent dies and a new child is born. It is a familiar cycle. Even though familiar, death is always mourned, even knowing of the new life to come. What must die in you in order for something new to take its place? Passivity? Politeness? Fear of rejection? Pride? Love of material things?

Examine your feelings and then write a gravestone epitaph for it.

Here Lies....

After the Funeral

The sea gull made me yawn, the way

> it

> st
> re
> t
> ch
> ed

> its

> chin,

trying to relax, feeling the weight
of what it had just swallowed.

❈

Afterward

What does the fish represent in Christianity? What does it feel like to swallow the fish? What does it have to do with death? How do you feel after a funeral of a loved one? How do you get rid of the feeling of the "weight of" what you "just swallowed"? How long do you expect it will take to grieve? Do you feel as if part of you has died as well? How will you grieve that?

Meditate on the Mt 28:20 scripture, "And remember, I am with you always, to the end of the age." How is God with you? Is there something of your loved one with you as well?

Write a poem entitled *At The End of the Earth*.

VI. GOD, WHAT IS GOOD GRIEF?

God will have compassion according to the abundance of steadfast love;
for God does not willingly afflict or grieve anyone.
Lamentations 3: 32

Dear God of Hope,

What can you tell me about this grief I feel? Why does loss always seem to come in multiples? How can

I discover the hope you offer while in the midst of loss? Give me the words to express my deepest

feelings for myself and others. Allow my pain to be transformed into words of hope and healing.

Amen.

Sisters

Four friends at a kitchen table
sit in unstuffed chairs,
straight-backed and honest,

say a few prayers, sing songs,
stay for hours allowing music
like deep breathing

to enter inner spaces.
Harmony and poetry
bind them as sisters,

four at a table, friends.
Each moment, held, not
advanced, unwilling to dance

forward, to friendships stretched
across continents, to tables
of broken bread and wine,

not knowing if time will lead
to music and poetry
more perfect than this.

The Grief of Moving Away

Have you experienced emotional intimacy? With whom? What does it feel like? In the poem four women friends sit at a table, not wanting to leave, because one of then was about to move away, breaking their "perfect" time together. Have you ever grieved the loss of a friend, not to death, but to a long distance move? How did that feel? Do you still keep in touch? What did you learn from that friend? Do our "perfect" times reveal anything to us about spiritual intimacy? Anything about God?

Write a poem entitled *More Perfect Than This.*

Estate Sale

Musty mink collars on coats of wool
emit bursts of musk when jostled.

Her silver, sparse and unmatched, her china,
chipped, show she had lived too long alone

in the white house across the street
where no one entered but the "go-for" man.

Last Christmas carolers sang outside
while she watched from her darkened den

and made no room at the inn for song,
nor light to brighten the dark night.

Now I watch the hunter-gatherers
shuffling treasures in and out

like tribes of hungry ants carrying
burdens too heavy for their frame.

They crawl over tatted lace,
framed photos of yellowed faces,

carnival glass, too gaudy
to use with formal china,

Reader's Digest classics, and
faded, embroidered sheets.

A sleek woman parks
a Jaguar adjacent to the sale.

She paws her way in,
surveys the territory,

then argues over a fur coat,
jumping at the jugular,

throwing coins, running
over ants, consuming the past.

The Loss of What We Have Accumulated

Everyone understands the emotional toll of loss due to death. Some understand loss due to divorce. But how many understand the emotional turmoil due to loss of job, loss of home or community, and especially loss of dreams? Have you ever been to an estate sale and tried to piece together who might have lived there and what their life was all about? Have you ever cried while watching greedy buyers fighting over intimate lace cloths or silk slips? What have you accumulated in your life that is important to you? If a fire broke out in your home today, what would you rescue, and what would you let burn? What dream have you lost? How and why? Has the dream been replaced? Have you grieved the loss?

Think of a character in the Bible who experienced a loss. Study that story and write about how he/she handled it. What does it tell you about your life and losses?

Looking for Normal

I'm in a tizzy,
forever busy.
Deadlines are past
but I'm still on *fast,*
still in shock,
around the clock.
I take cold showers
every two hours.
I eat chocolate bars
and play my guitar.
I go out to lunch
with the "old bunch"
but I'm not hungry.
I'm much too angry.
So I play loud music,
please excuse it,
and read a book, but
my brain won't look.
I take a fast walk
but I need to talk.
No one understands.
I wring my hands.
I want to scream, "I'm
stuck in a bad dream."
It's all too formal.
I need normal.
Where'd it go?
I'm desperate to know.
It's time to move on.
Normal's gone.

What is Normal?

This poem was written about the way many of us feel when we are grieving a loss. Any loss is associated with enormous stress, and stress can cause numerous negative outcomes, such as becoming accident prone and/or forgetful, and can cause word and thought blocking, and general brain fatigue. No wonder "normal" seems more like wonderful. But what is normal? After a loss will "normal" be the same as it used to be, or do you need to find a new "normal"? What will never be "normal" again? Let's call the new "normal" LAMRON, that's "normal" backwards.

Begin to describe what LAMRON will be. Can you see it beginning to take shape? How did the disciples establish LAMRON after Jesus' crucifixion?

<u>My LAMRON</u>

Comfort Food

I cook potato soup in November.
and remember how its starch
holds together dark nights.

I bake bread when I'm cold.
Its yeast unfolding in my brain
recalls loaf-warm kitchens.

I make popcorn when I'm lonely,
each pop, not only food
but brilliant movement.

I drink cocoa when I'm rejected,
its warm sweetness protecting
my every need.

I eat oatmeal each morning,
each warm grain warning:
I am ready.

Seeking Comfort

What do you do to pamper yourself? When life wields an arrow at you how do you duck?

This poem describes the concept of comfort food, food that relaxes your body as well as your soul. What foods do you associate with warm home kitchens, or earthy smells, or Grandma's dining room? When you are sick do you reach for chicken soup, or 7UP, or red jello? Do you relax when you smell home-made bread baking in the oven? We can get in trouble if we concentrate on these foods in exclusion of other, healthier foods, but once in a while they serve the purpose of helping us heal.

List your comfort foods. What associations do you have with them? What associations do you think Jesus had with unleavened bread and wine at Passover? What are your associations with bread and wine (or grape juice) at communion services?

Write a poem entitled *Each Warm Grain Warning*.

Sea Glass

Dust to dust
sand to sand
glass returns
from the sea
changed

This piece found
on a walk
on a day when
I was looking
down

Tired of shells
tired of sand
dragging my body
along a going-nowhere
beach

I spotted faint pink
of returned glass
frosted
by vicious
waves

Had it been
a bottle of
French perfume
flung overboard
in storm?

A glass tray
broken? A
bottle of lotion
emptied and
worthless?

Water broke it
slashed it
grated it on shells
then spit it
out

Like Jonah
on the beach
finally doing
what he was
told

Warming
in sunlight
above the
dead, strewn
shells

His face toward
Nineveh
his will
worked over
and worn

Becoming
one with
the white,
white
sand

⚜

Worked Over and Worn

Have you ever felt like a piece of sea glass, tossed, grated, sanded, flipped, washed, and then coming out as someone you hardly recognize? What happens to sea glass in the process? What happens to its sharp edges? Is that a loss or a gain? What happens to a person's ego during grief? What happens to a person's ability to control during a loss? What happens to the idea of safety? What does the last line mean, "Becoming one with the white, white sand"? What stage are you at in your grief? Are you still a sharp, broken piece of glass? Are you in the process of being "worked over and worn"? Are you "one with the white, white sand"?

Visualize a piece of sea glass and then write about your own stage of grief.

VII.   GOD, INSTRUCT ME IN THE WAYS OF PEACE AND JUSTICE

"When was it that we saw you hungry and gave you food, or thirsty and gave you something to drink? And when was it that we saw you a stranger and we welcomed you, or naked and gave you clothing? And when was it that we saw you sick or in prison and visited you?" And the sovereign will answer them, "Truly, I tell you, just as you did it to one of the least of these who are members of my family, you did it to me."
Matthew 25:37-40

Dear God of the sick and the lame, the naked and the poor,

the imprisoned, hungry and war-torn...

Help me to look into the eyes of those who suffer in this world, and not turn my face. Help me to do the things which work for peace and justice. Help me take violence and divert it into stewardship. Help me take suffering and turn it into understanding. Give me insight. Give me strength. Give me words to describe and to transform. And through it all give me the grace not to judge, but to love, the grace to feel but not to become paralyzed, and the grace to walk side by side with adversity.

Amen.

Christmas Child

I remember a Vietnam War vet who couldn't forget what he learned.
Saw too well where hell stood, close enough to be smuggled in by dog,
child or woman: hell lurking at fence-end, between rows of a green field,
outside an open window, by the mailbox, in his guts.

I listened to him

one Christmas morning muttering how he threw away
his Shetland-pony-and-picket-fence life, his wife, kid and farm
where he had it made, land paid for, and even the friendship of old
hometown folks who never forgot his touchdown on Homecoming.

Now I am like him.

Can't sit with my back to a window or drive to the grocer's
after dark. Can't control my heart's pounding as I hear a car approach.
I choose not to plug in Christmas! red! blinking! lights!
and I distrust guardian angels who sing of peace.

I cannot forget.

I still see the car rounding my street, screeching its brakes, a thief
demanding Christmas money, the hands of a child jerking a silver gun,
holding it to my face, twitching, holding it like something hot --
blinding in intensity, brilliant as the Christmas star,

but much, much closer.

❀

Peace on Our Streets

Is it possible? Have you ever been robbed? Have you ever had a gun held to your head? Did it change your worldview? What happens to your old fuzzy "give peace a chance" naivete? Is peace a naïve wish? In what way did Jesus say he was bringing peace to the world? Have you ever worked for peace? In what way? Jesus said, "Blessed are the peacemakers." (Matthew 5:9)

How can we work for peace, a realistic, lasting peace, in our homes, on our streets, in our country and in our world? Write a prose poem about your efforts, or your proposed efforts. (To write a prose poem you put your pen on the paper and keep writing until you are finished. Instead of using periods, you write commas, and keep on writing until your entire thought is finished. Prose poems contain a lot of detail.)

<u>Much, Much Closer</u>

Park and Shop

(my son noticed that 'Park and Shop'
backwards spells 'pohs and krap')

At the Park and Shop
you come to be seen.
You come to pose in clothes
with the right labels and step
inside to shelves of crap,
cigarettes, booze, stems of
75 cent satin roses with
cardboard heart and space to
sign your name or your X.

At the Park and Shop
iron bars protect windows
with faded pictures of
half nude ladies and their
Johnny Walker Red posing
for cowboys in jeans tight
enough to make them sterile.
Here they sell rolls of lotto
tickets, used ones underfoot,
all hope of winning gone.

Life's a gamble.
At night patron's designer
label jackets hide bullets
and guns, no turn of the bin
for winners and losers,
just a turn of the barrel
determines who gets
trampled underfoot
at the Park and Shop.

Violence

How do we work for peace and justice in a violent world? Is violence so much a part of human nature that it will never leave us? What did Jesus do in the face of violence? What did Martin Luther King Jr. do in the face of violence? What have you done in the face of a bully? What does turning the other cheek mean for us? Is it possible? Could it work? This poem talks about certain individuals who lead violent lives. Is there also a whole culture of violence? Are there violent nations? Does our nation condone violence? Do our families condone violence? Does your church condone violence? In what way?

Think about the words you use. Do you unconsciously use the metaphors of violence? (ex: Onward Christian soldiers marching as to war.) Do we cover up our violent intentions by changing the names of things? (ex: the defense department is actually the department of war.) Do you unconsciously use behaviors that can be interpreted as violent? (ex: spanking a child.)

Write a poem in response and use as many "v" words as possible:

Violence is Non-Viable

Beneath the Sick-A-War Tree

Your sycamore branches, thick with hearted leaves,
don't cool a northerner in your smothering shade.

Beneath this canopy of southern hospitality
no grass grows, your heart allows only filtered light.

My child plays under your care, feels your burden
and names you *Sick-A-War*. We do not feel safe here.

I cannot explain my fast-paced voice, my choices,
my immigrant name, in this plantation world.

I am haunted by swaying limbs, and bodies who swung there,
whose color was wrong or whose lips would not keep silent.

I tred softly on your prickly soil, aware of land mines,
fallen seedballs, protecting your birthright with affliction.

❧

Strangers

Moses said to his people, "You shall also love the stranger, for you were strangers in the land of Egypt." (Dt. 10:19) Seems logical, doesn't it? But have you ever been the "stranger"? Strangers can be identified by skin color, type of hair, or hair-do, clothing, diet, habits, religious beliefs, values, language, way of speaking, and even by the use of certain jargon terms. Think about the inhuman names we give to people we are at war with. It's easy to dehumanize the "stranger" who doesn't act as we do. We can be strangers within our own families between generations, between sexes. When have you been a stranger? What were the subtle differences that made you stand out? How did you overcome them? Are you still a stranger in a strange land? Is that a blessing, a mixed blessing, or a curse? What did you learn from being the stranger? How will you treat others because of it?

Write a limerick about a stranger:

There was a young ...   from ...

At the Movie

He says *What's in your purse?* between the chase scene
and the love scene on the big screen. *I'm hungry, got any food?*

As quietly as I can I send my hand into the wasteland of my purse,
combing through shredded Kleenex and sticky pennies,

rubber bands, brushes and keys. He knows I will find food.
He sees the crackers I sneak into my pocket as we leave the cafe,

the starlight mints I graciously accept, and never eat,
but store away in the bottom shelves of this purse.

And there are peanut M and M's just in case
I get caught in traffic and don't get home for lunch,

I can munch on protein and chocolate and survive
another hour in this hungry transitional place.

I hand him a Tootsie Roll. *Left from Halloween* I say,
and he winks and knows it is a life-saving purse,

carrying food which does not spoil, a loyal purse which
ensures against the bare cupboards of childhood.

Hunger

What are you doing about hunger in the world? Jesus said, "Feed my lambs." (Jn 21:15) Is there hunger in your own community? Do you help at a soup kitchen, a food closet? Do you belong to lobbying organizations such as Bread for the World? Do you write your political leaders and tell them to vote for hunger issues? Do you judge people at the grocery store who use food stamps? Have you ever been hungry?

Try fasting for a day, and then write about the experience.

<u>When the Hunger Pangs Start</u>

Mother

In Iraq today a soldier died. Flags wave, fireworks are shooting,
while classmates grieve in his old room, and his father talks of duty.
I imagine his mother doesn't talk at all. She deeply aches, and cries.

Yesterday boiling water killed a child. Today his father jailed, denies
it was deliberate, while police keep peace and lawyers practice law.
I imagine the child's mother doesn't talk at all. She deeply aches, and cries,

and pretends she holds her child once more, his beating heart against her own.
Whatever cause it was wasn't worth this pain. She wipes her darkened eyes.
And Mother doesn't talk at all. She deeply aches, and cries.

❧

Abuse

Is there anything you can do to prevent abuse and neglect? The poem talks about "the police keep peace and lawyers practice law," but what about you? Are tears enough? Is there an organization in your community that works for prevention of abuse and neglect? How can you help them?

In this poem called "Mother" the last line says "Mother deeply aches and cries." Could this be a reference to God? What is your understanding of the relationship of God to God's people?

Write a poem entitled *Through Darkened Eyes.*

Tomatoes in Cages

This spring there's a war going on,
and signs, letters, calls, poems, not even new life
bursting from the soil, can turn it off.

I plant seeds, water them well, plan each row
for color and space, place tomatoes in cages
and bind beans to their poles.

In the garage I dig my hands
into a dirty box and find the clipper
sharpened last fall, ready for combat.

Euonymous is first, too full and lush.
Its bush covers my lilies. I snip. I prune. I slash.
I clip. I sculpt. I amputate its invading limbs,

Then boxwood, holly, azalea,
prickly pyrocantha, bridal wreath …
even the graceful, white, bridal wreath.

I cut. I slash. I amputate
any spring growing thing in my way.
There is a war going on.

War

Do you believe that war is moral? Do you believe that if certain conditions are met then war is moral? Do you get caught up in the language and hype of war? Are you tolerant of people who feel different from you about this subject? Have you ever lost a loved one to war, or fought in a war yourself? This poem shows how a cultural feeling can develop where it seems all right to "cut, slash and amputate." How does that happen? Is there a way to stay outside of the cultural norms? How do we remain, or become, blessed peacemakers?

Write a poem entitled *Taking Tomatoes Out of Their Cages.*

VIII.   GOD, TEACH ME ABOUT THE EARTH

God saw everything that God had made, and indeed, it was very good.
Genesis 1:31

Dear God of Creation,

I share this earth with all kinds of critters and flowers, bugs and stones, rivers and clouds, each of them changing, moving at its own pace, in its own unique consciousness. Help me to understand this earth, not as my playground, but as my home, my community which deserves care and love. As I write poems about parts of this world give me better understanding of its interconnectedness with all creation, of its beauty, and its vulnerability. I am humble in the sight of this awesome creation.

Amen.

Names

The Asplundh tree man,
sinewy, with bark-tanned face,
calls me Ma'am

Doesn't know I am a Swede
same as Mr. Asplundh,
doesn't know my name

He asks me to sign
to clear cut my trees which
dare hang over Swepco wires

I won't sign,
make him show me the limbs
he is required to cut

I listen all day to buzzing
and watch the trees,
listen for the whine of the wind

Then head my wheelbarrow
for piles of broad limbs
just right for my fireplace

He says, *This is junk,
can't burn pine,
don't waste your time*

I load a white log and say,
This is river birch,
he shrugs his shoulders

I pick up poplar, oak
more river birch
and a little pine won't hurt

He thinks they are the same,
trees, just trees,
to cut out of the way

Like cancer
or a poison ivy vine
that chokes out life

His nametag says Mr. Brown,
but he does not know me
and he does not know the trees

And he does not know Mr. Asplundh
the Swede from Chicago
who called tree limbs "quist"

And he does not know
that in Mr. Asplundh's tongue
my name* means "blooming limb"

*Blomquist

Knowing Creation

Do you know the names of the trees in your yard? How about the names of the wildflowers that bloom in your ditch before they are mowed down? Do you know the names of the birds sitting on the telephone wire? If you choose to learn their names, then you will also have to look at them closer, and see their differences, their unique beauties. Every detail of God's creation is stunning. If you look closer you will feel awe.

Take an afternoon or morning and go to a wild area (or park) near your home. Observe nature. Take notes. Later look up what you did not know. As you watched the tiniest ants in their organized community, or the largest woodpecker drumming on a tree, or you saw a hummingbird draw nectar from an orange trumpet vine, did you feel the presence of God there? Did you hear "the still small voice of calm?" What are you doing to protect God's creation?

Write a poem entitled *The Voice of Calm*.

Think Globally: Act Locally

The CEO of Chemlawn has a mansion with
a yard green and smooth as a velveteen frog.
I don't run in his circles, but my dog and I jog
twice a day past his green expanse of grass,
which sprouts no weeds, wildflowers or dried
forgotten leaves, and upon which I only
occasionally allow my dog to run in his own
little circles, and then eliminate elegantly.
We should avoid trespassing at times when
tiny printed signs are posted: *Caution:*
Lawn chemicals have been applied,
but I know, with the help of my dog, that spots
of darker, taller grass or yellowed circles,
like landings of tiny UFO's, will emerge
even though chemicals try their best
to equalize and maximize. My eyes watch
for dog-inspired art, while my lips whistle
a tune which even velveteen frogs
should know: *It's not that easy being*
green. Why? Wonder why?

Taking Care of the Earth

Do lawn chemicals make a better earth, or a less healthy earth? Is this a black and white issue, or is there a middle ground? Do you think about how big a footprint you are making on the earth, and if the earth can survive it? What can you do as a home-owner to take care of the earth? What can you do as a consumer of goods? Traditionally Christianity has not said a lot about caring for the earth. When Christians started asking about the subject, it was relegated to the area of stewardship. God gave this land to us, and we need to be good stewards of it. But let's go a step further. What if God gave this land to all its inhabitants for safe keeping, not just to the humans? We know we share the earth with other creatures, creatures that we are just beginning to understand. Think about taking care of the earth as a fellow creature, not as the king of creatures. How does that change your perception?

The above poem was written with a sense of humor. Write a humorous poem about sharing the earth with all creatures (and rocks and minerals as well.)

It's Not That Easy Being . . .

Upgrading MN State Highway #95

Red flags dot our village entrance,
Red flags among the moccasin flower,
Towering pines, ice cream signs,

Flags that touch but do not hear
Silent pealing of bluebells
Or Jack praying in the pulpit

Because of pounding noise
Of cars that pass too fast
With destinations unclear.

Red flags lack clean white
And river blue of the flag that flies
At our village hall.

They clash with history
And fashion progress
In their own modern image.

A red flag village cannot rest.
The eagle's nest has been found
And fragile unity of history and ground,

Of village as giver of life
Is wound with cobweb silk
to serenity's elusive sound.

❧

Progress?

Have you ever been in a town or city or county that wanted to bulldoze your favorite wild area, or historic site? What did you do? Did it work? Or have you been the "progressive" one who does not understand those who stand in the way of "growth?" Is there a way to talk to one another? What should the issues be? What "red flags" does it raise?

Write about your experience in terms of preserving all of Gods creatures and creation. Write a poem entitled *Not Another Jericho*.

Under Nature's Wing

Tripping on a downed wire fence I land snow-ward
Cowardly whining words of defeat.

While off balance a shadow covers this carcass.
Circling down, examining that wounded sound,

An eagle pierces my eye, intense with the hunt,
Sensing vulnerability.

But my eye too carries power, dares to stare
Back, challenging the towering bird.

This union shared of momentary insight
Continues creating a bond of being

Strong as a baby's gaze into
Its mother's eyes at birth,

A bond of seeing under nature's wing
A fleeting glimpse, and freeing.

❈

A New Vision

Have you had an experience in nature that has been a way of "seeing under nature's wing a fleeting glimpse, and freeing"? Pretend you have just taken off your dark glasses (seeing in a mirror dimly) and put on powerful new lenses that let you see as good as a cat, hear as wonderfully as a bat, see the ultra-violet colors as a housefly does, and pick up scents as brilliantly as a dog.

Write about wearing these lenses.

A New Vision

Snowy Morning in Oklahoma

Like white chocolate on mixed nuts
the snow coats this crazy world
and makes it sweet.

I open my morning shade, spy
the sparse white snow.
My body sighs.

It is an old feeling, from cold
northern winters, when this
blanket of white

reflected the half light of a
low lying sun, and told my
eyes to blink.

On mornings of white I do not
think. I allow my breath
to slow.

This snow, this breath, this
moment. I blink, I sigh,
I know.

Meditating in Nature

Do you take time to breathe deeply and allow the creation to seep into your consciousness? How do you stop your thinking? What calming words do you say to yourself as you deep-breathe? Try saying the words from Ps 118:24, "This is the day the Creator has made. Let us rejoice and be glad in it." What happens when you fully connect with Mother Earth (God)? What do the words "I know" in the last line mean?

Write a poem entitled *I Know*.

IX. GOD OF RITUALS AND SEASONS

For everything there is a season, and a time for every matter under heaven.
Ecclesiastes 3:1

Dear God Who Loves the Church and Its People,

Your church helps me organize my life into times of creation and new life, times of repentance, times of praise, times of celebration, and times of remembrance. Each day of the church calendar gives me a new challenge as I say, "This is the day the Creator has made. Let us rejoice and be glad in it."

Bless each season. Bless each day.

Bless each moment.

Amen.

At Christmas

It's the only time of year I wear red, the obvious color,
loved by everyone. They say it favors me, matches
the spider veins of my cheeks, like Santa's,
or the glowing nose of Rudolph.

I prefer orange, the hated color of Halloween and 60's carpet,
but I take out red at Christmas when the world
turns white and only evergreens
display their color.

I wear Christmas crimson – not as some rite of blood shed,
but because I remember how a baby's cheeks
turn red with crying, with cold,
with warm holding.

A baby's lips turn red with sucking, and babbling, and
its toes glow positively rose while kicking
at the air, pumping blood into
precise paths.

It's not the sacrifice I reflect in my red turtle-necks
and Christmas plaid slacks, no, it's the
newly-born flesh, flushed with
rushing life.

What Does Christmas Mean to You?

Everyone has such different dreams, expectations, traditions and ideas about Christmas that it is an intensely personal holiday. If you take the cultural traditions away, what is left for you? What does Jesus birth mean? Is it in some ways a celebration of all life, of all Creation? Do you agree with the poem, or disagree?

Write a rhyming Christmas card to yourself about what you believe.

Marked

Did you know
they hanged girls
who had moles,

thought it
marked them
as a witch

in Salem, Massachusetts
three hundred
years ago?

And if you said,
*I didn't ask
for moles,*

they still believed
you were marked
as evil.

People with moles
are scary, different.
They're witches,

and no matter
what you wish
only decades of time

will change
their minds.
Moles don't

go away, don't
fade like freckles.
They mark you.

❧

Ash Wednesday

Women don't choose to be female, although most wouldn't change that if they could. They are marked as female. Any woman could shave her head and flatten her breasts, but there is something inside which marks her as a woman. The same goes for men. There are also markers other than gender ones. In the poem villagers used moles as a mark of a witch. The Amish dress differently as a mark of their non-worldliness. People in India used to wear caste marks on their foreheads to alert others of their social status.

On Ash Wednesday we choose to be marked with the cross of Christ, to wear it on our foreheads to alert others of our Christian heritage.

What does being marked with the cross of Christ mean? Write a poem entitled *I Choose to be Marked*.

I Hear Grandma Laughing

This birth month, April, never brought you laughter.
Spring meant long days of hoeing and planting, sewing for Easter,

filling pots and bowls of food for teams of hired men, tired,
hungry from working and warming newly-thawed earth.

You could have celebrated with us today, cheered and sung,
but you chose to stop eating four years ago, said farewell

to your children, grand and great-grand, farewell to your
strawberries and roses, and to your window wall of violets.

If you were here today I know you would shush the singing,
re-cork the bottle, accept only gifts of flowers and food

and we would remark how your longevity is due
to hard work, no pampering, and oatmeal each morning.

In today's thaw I cannot stay inside, my window of violets
pales at the sight of azalea hills in this Oklahoma town,

alongside redbud and dogwood, their blossoms lovely
as the baby blankets you quilted from left-over flannel.

Can you see these southern flowers through my eyes,
blooms that never flourished in the cold nights and

short summers of Minnesota? For you survival in a
northern climate negated all forms of frivolous life.

I hear your voice, your laughter, (How could it be
laughter, you never laughed?) but I hear it plain,

and now again. I stare at crimson tulips transported
on vessels from overseas, blooming in this foreign soil.

As your mother before you survived the tall ship journey,
your laughter navigates across the expanse of time,

and I understand how it is possible to transplant joy
to one another on this day in April, a day of budding.

Easter

"A day of budding." Is that what Easter is? This is a resurrection poem, a poem of new life after death. Does God ever speak to you through laughter? Through spring flowers? How is it possible to "transplant joy to one another"? Imagine the garden of joy, and begin digging up your tulip bulb to transplant. What does that garden look like, smell like, feel like? How much fertile loam will you bring with your bulb?

Where will you plant it? How will you take care of it? Write a poem entitled *Transplanting Joy.*

Light and Shadow

It's July in Oklahoma. In Tulsa they call it Green Country,
but not this summer of 100 degree heat when

stroke killed men working and walking outside.
Still I walk to the river in search of the only breeze.

The trees between here and there shelter me from the sun
and keep my feet moving though they feel like heavy water,

about to explode. A faint smell of creosote greets me
at the abandoned railroad bridge, gathering place of walkers,

fisher people and breeze-wishers. An old cowboy stroking
a long beard says, *I ain't been et yet,* and points down

to fish swimming in the low water, schools of shiners
chased by bass and crappie, bass and crappie chased by gar,

all on the move, racing in spurts to survive another day
in the clear, shallow waters at the foot of the river dam.

A child watches as her mother sends out fish line.
There's a big, big one over there, Mama, and her mama looks

and grumbles because she sees no fish at all, only
something squeezing through the shade, a fish of light,

not moving, not struggling, not eating, not being eaten,
a length of sunlight, playing with the water, alive only to the child.

Her mama says nothing. This mirage will not catch her hook,
will not fill her hungry belly, nor cool her salty face.

It continues to hold its place against rock, debris and dam.
This light, trickster of children and old cowboys,

is a breeze-wisher, I know, because I see it floating,
flapping like a flag in the watery reflection of the sky.

❧

Pentecost

On this holy day Christians celebrate the descent of the holy spirit (the descending dove) onto the disciples. In this poem a young girl sees a light on the water and interprets it as a fish (an early symbol of Christianity.) The poet calls the light a "breeze-wisher." The old Hebrew word "ruach" means "breath," "wind," "spirit," "holy spirit." Is this fish of light "ruach"? Why doesn't the mother appreciate the fish? At what times in your life have you felt "Pentecost" happening to you? Do you have to be a "Pentecostal" in order to feel it?

Write a poem entitled *Breeze Wisher.*

Baptism

The water is clear,
no color yet reflected
from this new life,
until cheeks redden
and lips turn purple.
A child, who seeks
only comfort and peace,
cries, as a cold cross is
drawn on her brow, then
gently wiped dry with
Grandmother's lace cloth,
white, pure, absorbing all.

Renewing Your Baptism

Has your life been re-consecrated? In whose arms are you being held? What does the phrase "Grandmother's lace cloth, white, pure, absorbing all" mean to you? Water is the prime symbol in our human life because without it, we cannot survive. It hydrates us, as well as cleans us. What does water mean to you? Is there a body of water that is meaningful to you, a lake, a creek, a river, an ocean? How often do you go there? Do you have any simple rituals when you go there? Do you feel cleansed when you return?

Next time bring back an object from the water and place it in your home. When you look at it or touch it, remember the life-giving, cleansing waters of baptism, and the gentle wiping with the handkerchief by a Loved One. Write a poem entitled *Cross and Cloth*.

Moving On

I once lived
in a century
old house

       where creaking walls
       conjured dreams
       of dead farmers

who starved
growing corn
on its sand hills

       but stayed around
       to see how it all
       turned out -

the hundred acres
now carved into fives,
houses sprouting

       on drives
       meandering over
       hills of sand.

Ghost farmers
disappeared when
stacked stone homes

       dwarfed the old house
       and bluestem prairie
       gave way to lawn.

Cedars I planted
years ago are
all that's left

       of wild. Pines
       and subdivisions
       thrive on

       hills of sand,
       but I need
       more.

❧

But I Need More

When you examine your spirituality, does it seem as though something is missing? The answer may be NO. But for many women the answer is YES. There are few feminine models of the divine. Does that mean there are no feminine aspects of the divine? What do you think? How do you feel? Do you believe God is life-giving, nurturing, understanding, intimate? In your own life who most closely fits those characteristics, mother or father? Who bakes the *bread of life*? Who gives of her own body to nurse an infant?

Write about divine characteristics that appear to be feminine-like. What "hills of sand" do not support you any longer? Are you still looking for "more?"

<u>Hills of Sand</u>

Rising Backwards

When I learned to write my name it slanted backwards.
Even when Teacher slapped my knuckles the dancing
flow of letters filled a space no other writer owned
and no teacher could persuade me to abandon.

Later, I loved to study the reason ancient peoples
wrote on walls, and I loved to juggle geometric
puzzles, proving theorems back to their origin,
where thinking backwards was to my advantage.

When I bought my ten-speed bike I peddled
backwards, no gear to slow rotation,
flowing up and down like bubbling oil, the bike
didn't move, only my feet were in orbit.

And in tennis I win with a strong backhand.
Opponents try to outwit me by putting the ball
behind, but my mind is seldom in front
and my two-handed return is powerful.

I prefer the back of the bus where I feel bumps,
and I love the underbelly of my Victorian porch
in the cool, dog-haired dirt. It reminds me that
the flip side of life is most certainly not death.

It's more like getting chained into a forward seat
of a double ferris-wheel, then rising backwards
through enormous space, up and around,
my face coming last, surprised and weightless.

❈

141

Circle of Life

People may have told you that what you are, or do, is wrong – but you know better. Your peculiarities are God-given, and spirit-filled. Scientific chaos theory celebrates our differences as necessities for the survival of human life on earth. Sometimes it is our crazy nature, that part questioned by others, that actually leads us to spiritual understanding. How does the poet describe "The flip side of life?" Does the enormous circle that is described mean heaven? Could it mean a spiritual dimension of this life? How is this metaphor different from the Old (Hebrew) Testament's Jacob's ladder?

Write a poem entitled *The Flip Side.*

About the Author

Cynthia Gustavson was born in rural Minnesota to a jazz musician and a waitress in 1947. She is the author of five poetry collections, several poetry therapy workbooks, and has published in numerous journal articles. She was educated at Gustavus Adolphus College, Boston University, Louisiana State University, United Seminary of the Twin Cities, and Oklahoma State University, has taught at Northeastern State University in Tallequah, Oklahoma, and Louisiana State University in Shreveport, Louisiana, and has been an invited lecturer around the country.

In her twenty-two years as a social worker she has worked in drug prevention, practiced individual and group therapy, worked extensively with caregivers of the chronically ill and developmentally disabled.

Winner of a New Millennium Writings Award in 2002 and finalist for the Rita Dove Poetry Award from the Salem College Center for Women Writers in 2004, Gustavson lives and works in Tulsa, Oklahoma with her husband of 36 years.

More information can be found at www.cynthiagustavson.com